Alfred's Kid's Ukulele Course
Sacred Songbook

17 Fun Arrangements that Make Learning Even Easier!

Ron Manus • L.C. Harnsberger

Contents

* Alfred's Teach Your Child to Play Ukulele page references are shown at the bottom of each song title page.

Using the CD  TRACKS 1 & 2

The included **Alfred's Kid's Ukulele Course Sacred Songbook CD** contains all the songs in this book for listening and playing along. Use the first two tracks to get your ukulele in tune. Listen carefully to the instructions on track I, then use track 2 to match each string to the recorded pitch. Be sure to tune your ukulele every time you play, especially when you play along with the CD.

Produced by
Alfred Music
P.O. Box 10003
Van Nuys, CA 91410-0003
alfred.com

ISBN-10: 1-4706-1761-7 (Book & CD)
ISBN-13: 978-1-4706-1761-5 (Book & CD)

Cover illustrations by Jeff Shelly
CD performed by Jared Meeker

Amazing Grace

Track 3

Music by William Walker
Lyrics by John Newton

A - ma - zing Grace, how sweet the

sound, That saved a wretch like

C7

me. I once was

lost but now am found, Was

F

blind, but now I see.

* This music also correlates to Alfred's Teach Your Child to Play Ukulele, Book 1, p. 83.

Additional Lyrics

T'was Grace that taught my heart to fear.
And Grace, my fears relieved.
How precious did that Grace appear
The hour I first believed.

Through many dangers, toils and snares
I have already come;
'Tis Grace that brought me safe thus far
And Grace will lead me home.

The Lord has promised good to me.
His word my hope secures.
He will my shield and portion be,
As long as life endures.

Yea, when this flesh and heart shall fail,
And mortal life shall cease,
I shall possess within the veil,
A life of joy and peace.

God Is So Good

Track 4

Traditional

God is so good, _____ God is so good, _____

God is so good, He's so good to me! _____

Additional Lyrics

He cares for me,
He cares for me,
He cares for me,
He's so good to me!

I love Him so,
I love Him so,
I love Him so,
He's so good to me!

I praise His Name,
I praise His Name,
I praise His Name,
He's so good to me!

* This music also correlates to Alfred's Teach Your Child to Play Ukulele, Book 1, p. 83.

He's Got the Whole World in His Hands

Book 1, p. 42 (Complete, p. 67)*

Track 5

Traditional

Additional Lyrics

He's got the wind and the rain in His hands,
He's got the wind and the rain in His hands,
He's got the wind and the rain in His hands,
He's got the whole world in His hands.

He's got the tiny little baby in His hands,
He's got the tiny little baby in His hands,
He's got the tiny little baby in His hands,
He's got the whole world in His hands.

He's got you and me, brother, in His hands,
He's got you and me, brother, in His hands,
He's got you and me, brother, in His hands,
He's got the whole world in His hands.

He's got ev'rybody here in His hands,
He's got ev'rybody here in His hands,
He's got ev'rybody here in His hands,
He's got the whole world in His hands.

* This music also correlates to Alfred's Teach Your Child to Play Ukulele, Book 1, p. 83.

If You're Happy and You Know It

Book 2, p. 21 (Complete, p. 95)*

Track 6

Traditional

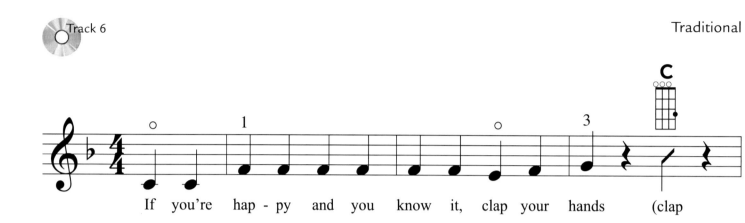

If you're hap - py and you know it, clap your hands   (clap

clap)   If you're hap - py and you know it, clap your hands   (clap

clap)   If you're hap - py and you know it, then your   face will sure - ly

show it   If you're hap - py and you know it clap your hands.   (clap   clap)

* This music also correlates to Alfred's Teach Your Child to Play Ukulele, Book 1, p. 39.

Additional Lyrics

If you're happy and you know it,
stomp your feet (stomp stomp)
If you're happy and you know it,
stomp your feet (stomp stomp)
If you're happy and you know it,
then your face will surely show it
If you're happy and you know it,
stomp your feet. (stomp stomp)

If you're happy and you know it,
shout "Hurray!" (hoo-ray!)
If you're happy and you know it,
shout "Hurray!" (hoo-ray!)
If you're happy and you know it,
then your face will surely show it
If you're happy and you know it,
shout "Hurray!" (hoo-ray!)

If you're happy and you know it,
do all three* (clap-clap, stomp-stomp, hoo-ray!)
If you're happy and you know it,
do all three (clap-clap, stomp-stomp, hoo-ray!)
If you're happy and you know it,
then your face will surely show it
If you're happy and you know it,
do all three. (clap-clap, stomp-stomp, hoo-ray!)

*For the last verse, play the chords six times instead of just twice so you play chords for clapping, stomping and hoo-raying!

I've Got Peace Like a River

Book 2, p. 35 (Complete, p. 115)*

Traditional

Track 7

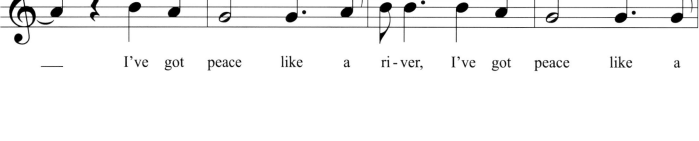

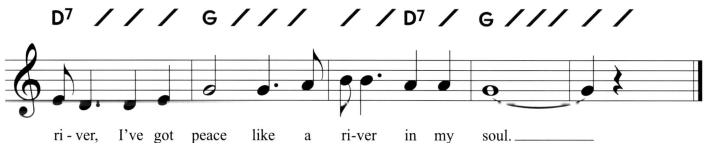

* This music also correlates to Alfred's Teach Your Child to Play Ukulele, Book 2, p. 63.

Additional Lyrics

I've got joy like a fountain,
I've got joy like a fountain,
I've got joy like a fountain in my soul.
I've got joy like a fountain,
I've got joy like a fountain,
I've got joy like a fountain in my soul.

I've got love like an ocean,
I've got love like an ocean,
I've got love like an ocean in my soul.
I've got love like an ocean,
I've got love like an ocean,
I've got love like an ocean in my soul.

I've got peace like a river,
I've got joy like a fountain,
I've got love like an ocean in my soul.
I've got peace like a river,
I've got joy like a fountain,
I've got love like an ocean in my soul.

I've Got the Joy, Joy, Joy, Joy

Track 8

Words and Music by
George Willis Cooke

I've got the joy, joy, joy, joy down in my heart, ____

Down in my heart, ____ Down in my heart, I've got the

joy, joy, joy, joy down in my heart, ____

Down in my heart, to stay. ____ And I'm so

Chorus

* This music also correlates to Alfred's Teach Your Child to Play Ukulele, Book 1, p. 83.

Additional Lyrics

I have the love of Jesus, love of Jesus, down in my heart,
Down in my heart,
down in my heart!
I have the love of Jesus, love of Jesus, down in my heart,
Down in my heart to stay!
CHORUS

I have the peace that passes understanding down in my heart,
I have the peace that passes understanding down in my heart,
Down in my heart,
down in my heart!
Down in my heart to stay.
CHORUS

I have the joy, joy, joy, joy down in my heart,
Down in my heart, down in my heart!
I have the joy, joy, joy, joy down in my heart,
Down in my heart to stay!
CHORUS

11

Jesus Loves Me

Track 9

Music by Anna B. Warner
Lyrics by William B. Bradbury

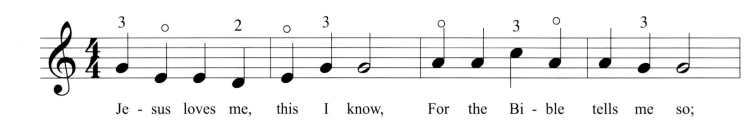

Je - sus loves me, this I know, For the Bi - ble tells me so;

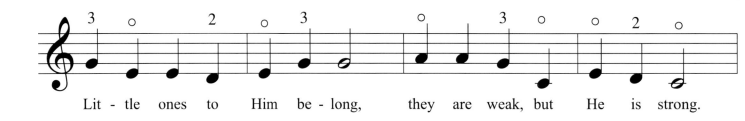

Lit - tle ones to Him be - long, they are weak, but He is strong.

Yes, Je - sus loves me, Yes, Je - sus loves me,

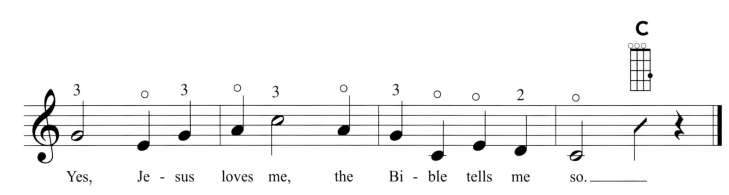

Yes, Je - sus loves me, the Bi - ble tells me so._____

* This music also correlates to Alfred's Teach Your Child to Play Ukulele, Book 1, p. 83.

Additional Lyrics

Jesus loves me, this I know,
As He loved so long ago,
Taking children on His knee,
Saying, "Let them come to Me."

REFRAIN:
Yes, Jesus loves me,
Yes, Jesus loves me,
Yes, Jesus loves me,
The Bible tells me so.

Jesus loves me still today,
Walking with me on my way,
Wanting as a friend to give
Light and love to all who live.
REFRAIN

Jesus loves me, He who died
Heaven's gate to open wide;
He will wash away my sin,
Let His little child come in.
REFRAIN

Jesus loves me, He will stay
Close beside me all the way;
Thou hast bled and died for me,
I will henceforth live for Thee.
REFRAIN

Joshua Fit the Battle of Jericho

Track 10

Traditional

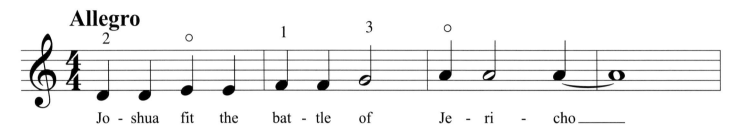

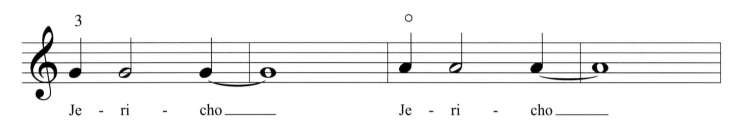

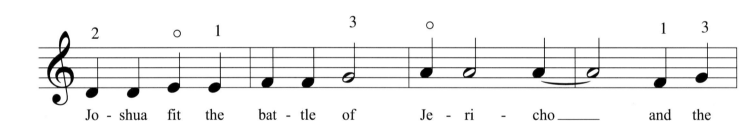

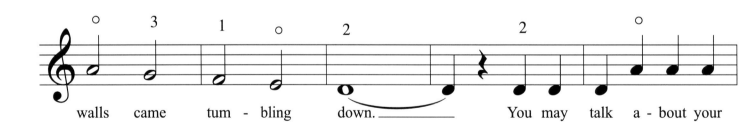

* This music also correlates to Alfred's Teach Your Child to Play Ukulele, Book 2, p. 55.

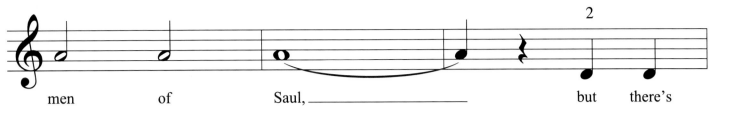

men   of   Saul, _____   but   there's

none   like   good   old   Jo - sh - ua _____   at   the

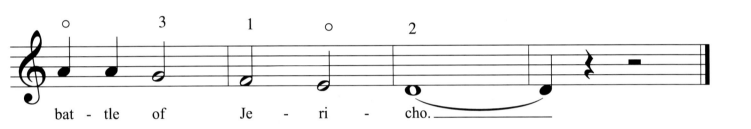

bat - tle   of   Je - ri - cho. _____

Additional Lyrics

Joshua fit the battle of Jericho,
Jericho, Jericho.
Joshua fit the battle of Jericho,
And the walls come tumbling down.

Up to the walls of Jericho,
With sword drawn in his hand.

Go blow them horns, cried Joshua,
The battle is in my hands.

Joshua fit the battle of Jericho,
Jericho, Jericho.
Joshua fit the battle of Jericho,
And the walls come tumbling down.

Joyful, Joyful, We Adore Thee

Book 1, p. 42 (Complete, p. 67)*

Track 11

Music by
Ludwig van Beethoven
Lyrics by
Henry Van Dyke

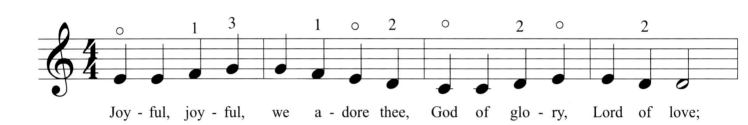

Joy - ful, joy - ful, we a - dore thee, God of glo - ry, Lord of love;

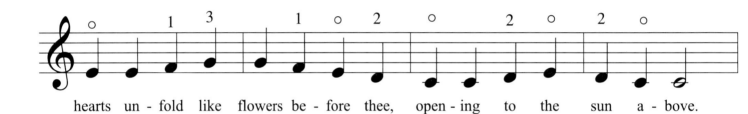

hearts un - fold like flowers be - fore thee, open - ing to the sun a - bove.

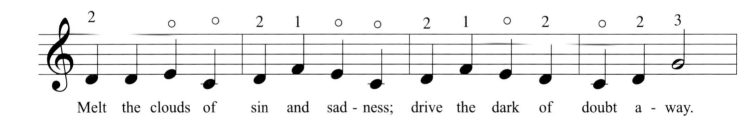

Melt the clouds of sin and sad - ness; drive the dark of doubt a - way.

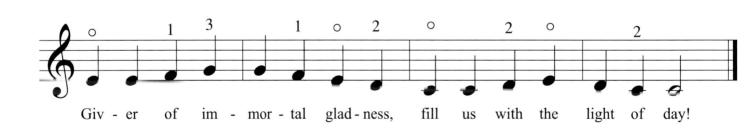

Giv - er of im - mor - tal glad - ness, fill us with the light of day!

* This music also correlates to Alfred's Teach Your Child to Play Ukulele, Book 1, p. 83.

Additional Lyrics

All Thy works with joy surround Thee,
Earth and heav'n reflect Thy rays,
Stars and angels sing around Thee,
Center of unbroken praise.
Field and forest, vale and mountain,
Flow'ry meadow, flashing sea,
Singing bird and flowing fountain
Call us to rejoice in Thee.

Thou art giving and forgiving,
Ever blessing, ever blest,
Wellspring of the joy of living,
Ocean depth of happy rest!
Thou our Father, Christ our Brother,
All who live in love are Thine;
Teach us how to love each other,
Lift us to the joy divine.

Mortals, join the happy chorus,
Which the morning stars began;
Father love is reigning o'er us,
Brother love binds man to man.
Ever singing, march we onward,
Victors in the midst of strife,
Joyful music leads us Sunward
In the triumph song of life.

Kum Ba Yah [Chord Version]

Track 12

Traditional

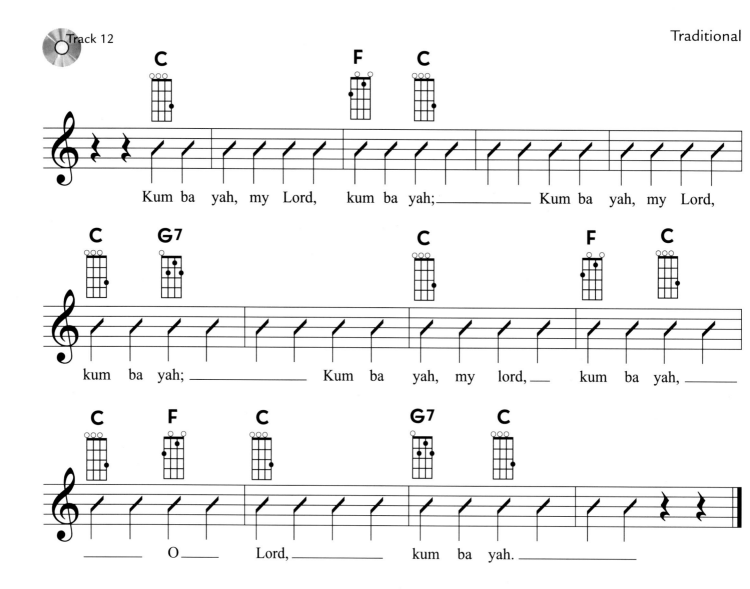

Kum ba yah, my Lord, kum ba yah;——— Kum ba yah, my Lord,

kum ba yah; ——— Kum ba yah, my lord,— kum ba yah,———

——— O ——— Lord,——— kum ba yah.———

Additional Lyrics

Someone's laughing, Lord, kum ba yah;
Someone's laughing, Lord, kum ba yah;
Someone's laughing, Lord, kum ba yah,
    O Lord, kum ba yah.

Someone's crying, Lord, kum ba yah;
Someone's crying, Lord, kum ba yah;
Someone's crying, Lord, kum ba yah,
    O Lord, kum ba yah.

Someone's praying, Lord, kum ba yah;
Someone's praying, Lord, kum ba yah;

Someone's praying, Lord, kum ba yah,
    O Lord, kum ba yah.

Someone's singing, Lord, kum ba yah;
Someone's singing, Lord, kum ba yah;
Someone's singing, Lord, kum ba yah,
    O Lord, kum ba yah.

Kum ba yah, my Lord, kum ba yah;
Kum ba yah, my Lord, kum ba yah;
Kum ba yah, my Lord, kum ba yah,
    O Lord, kum ba yah.

* This music also correlates to Alfred's Teach Your Child to Play Ukulele, Book 1, p. 41.

Kum Ba Yah [Melody Version]

Traditional

Track 13

Additional Lyrics

Someone's laughing, Lord, kum ba yah;
Someone's laughing, Lord, kum ba yah;
Someone's laughing, Lord, kum ba yah,
    O Lord, kum ba yah.

Someone's crying, Lord, kum ba yah;
Someone's crying, Lord, kum ba yah;
Someone's crying, Lord, kum ba yah,
    O Lord, kum ba yah.

Someone's praying, Lord, kum ba yah;
Someone's praying, Lord, kum ba yah;

Someone's praying, Lord, kum ba yah,
    O Lord, kum ba yah.

Someone's singing, Lord, kum ba yah;
Someone's singing, Lord, kum ba yah;
Someone's singing, Lord, kum ba yah,
    O Lord, kum ba yah.

Kum ba yah, my Lord, kum ba yah;
Kum ba yah, my Lord, kum ba yah;
Kum ba yah, my Lord, kum ba yah,
    O Lord, kum ba yah.

* This music also correlates to Alfred's Teach Your Child to Play Ukulele, Book 1, p. 83.

Michael, Row the Boat Ashore

Book 1, p. 42 (Complete, p. 67)*

Track 14

Traditional

Mi- chael row the boat a - shore, Hal - le - lu - jah! Mi- chael row the boat a - shore Hal - le - lu - - jah!_____

Additional Lyrics

Sister help to trim the sail,
Hallelujah!
Sister help to trim the sail,
Hallelujah!

Michael row the boat ashore,
Hallelujah!
Michael row the boat ashore,
Hallelujah!

* This music also correlates to Alfred's Teach Your Child to Play Ukulele, Book 1, p. 83.

Jordan's River is deep and wide,
Hallelujah!
Milk and honey on the other side,
Hallelujah!

Michael row the boat ashore,
Hallelujah!
Michael row the boat ashore,
Hallelujah!

Then you'll hear the trumpet sound,
Hallelujah!
Trumpet sound the world around,
Hallelujah!

Michael row the boat ashore,
Hallelujah!
Michael row the boat ashore,
Hallelujah!

Trumpet sound the jubilee,
Hallelujah!
Trumpet sound for you and me,
Hallelujah!

Michael row the boat ashore,
Hallelujah!
Michael row the boat ashore,
Hallelujah!

Nobody Knows the Troubles I've Seen

Traditional

Track 15

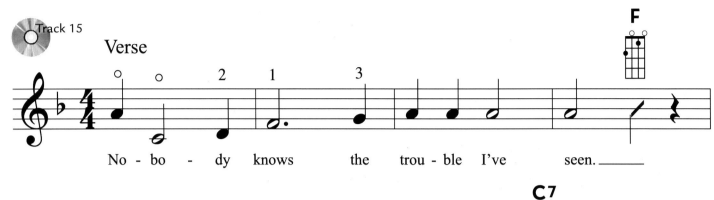

Verse

No - bo - dy knows the trou - ble I've seen. _____

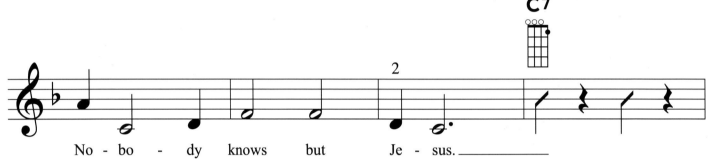

No - bo - dy knows but Je - sus. _____

No - bo - dy knows the trou - ble I've seen, _____

Chorus

glo - ry Hal - le - lu - jah! _____ Some -

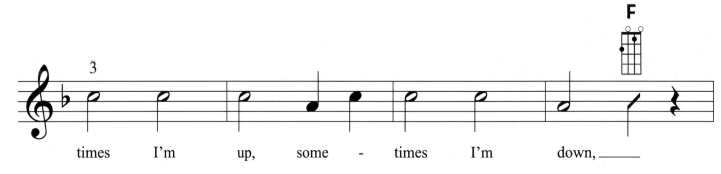

times I'm up, some - times I'm down, _____

* This music also correlates to Alfred's Teach Your Child to Play Ukulele, Book 2, p. 15.

oh, _____ yes, _____ Lord! _____ Some -

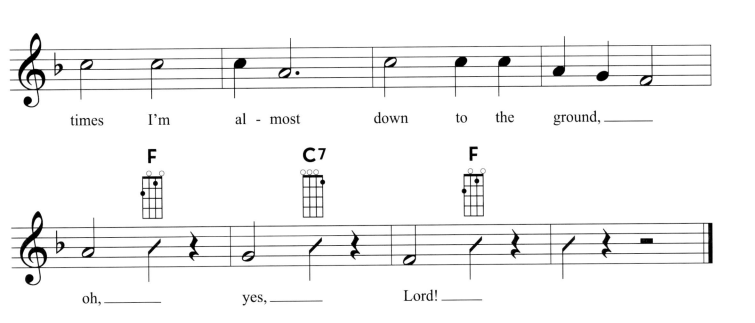

times I'm al - most down to the ground, _____

oh, _____ yes, _____ Lord! _____

Additional Lyrics

VERSE

Although you see me going 'long so,
Oh, yes, Lord,
I have my trials here below,
Oh, yes, Lord.

VERSE

If you get there before I do,
Oh, yes, Lord,
Tell all-a my friends I'm coming to Heaven!
Oh, yes, Lord.

VERSE

Onward, Christian Soldiers

 Track 16

Music by
Arthur Sullivan
Lyrics by
Sabine Baring-Gould

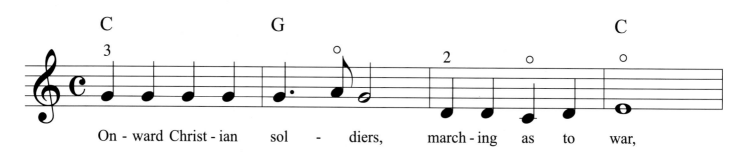

On - ward Christ - ian sol - diers, march - ing as to war,

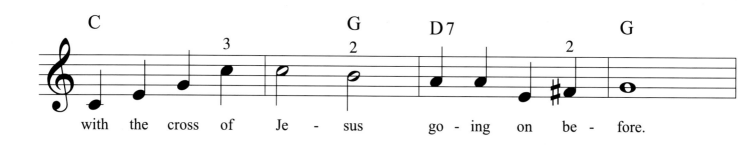

with the cross of Je - sus go - ing on be - fore.

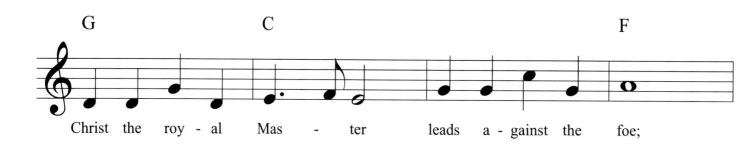

Christ the roy - al Mas - ter leads a - gainst the foe;

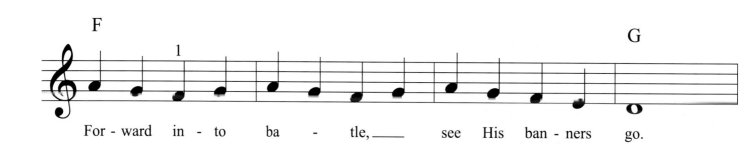

For - ward in - to ba - tle, ___ see His ban - ners go.

* This music also correlates to Alfred's Teach Your Child to Play Ukulele, Book 2, p. 65.

Refrain

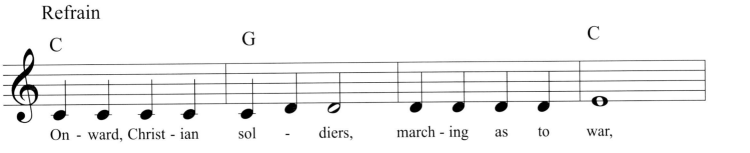

On - ward, Christ - ian sol - diers, march - ing as to war,

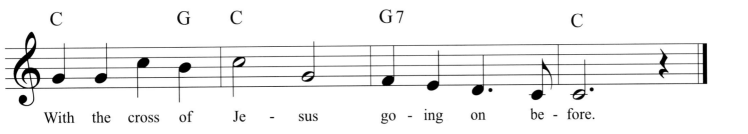

With the cross of Je - sus go - ing on be - fore.

Additional Lyrics

Crowns and thrones may perish,
Kingdoms rise and wane,
But the Church of Jesus
Constant will remain;
Gates of hell can never
'Gainst that church prevail;
We have Christ's own promise,
And that cannot fail.
REFRAIN

Onward, then, ye people!
Join our happy throng;
Blend with ours your voices
In the triumph song:
"Glory, laud and honor
Unto Christ the King!"
This through countless ages
We with angels sing.
REFRAIN

Shall We Gather at the River

Track 17

Music and lyrics by
Robert Lowry

C

Refrain

* This music also correlates to Alfred's Teach Your Child to Play Ukulele, Book 2, p. 15.

beau - ti - ful, the beau - ti - ful ___ ri - ver;

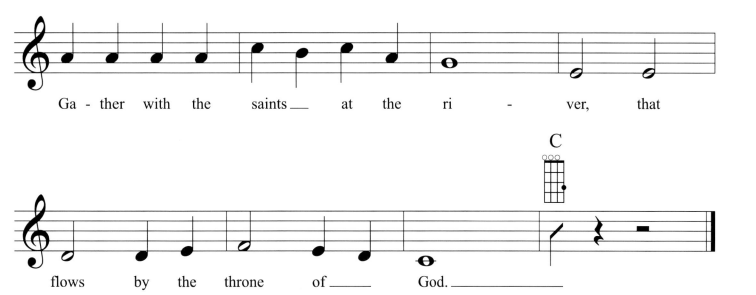

Ga - ther with the saints ___ at the ri - ver, that

C

flows by the throne of ___ God. ___

Additional Lyrics

On the margin of the river,
Washing up its silver spray,
We will walk and worship ever,
All the happy golden day.
REFRAIN

Ere we reach the shining river,
Lay we every burden down;
Grace our spirits will deliver,
And provide a robe and crown.
REFRAIN

Soon we'll reach the shining river,
Soon our pilgrimage will cease;
Soon our happy hearts will quiver
With the melody of peace.
REFRAIN

Swing Low, Sweet Chariot

Book 1, p. 42 (Complete, p. 67)*

Track 18

Traditional

* This music also correlates to Alfred's Teach Your Child to Play Ukulele, Book 1, p. 83.

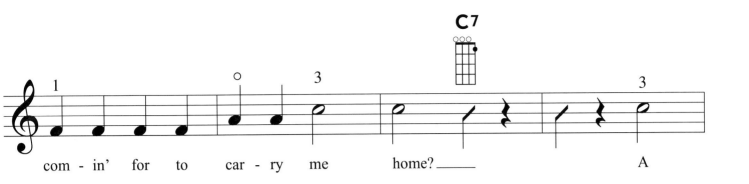

com - in' for to car - ry me home?_____ A

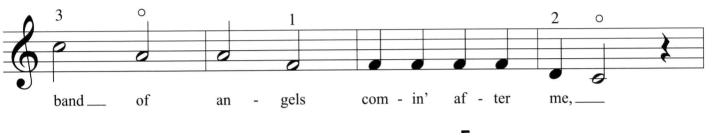

band__ of an - gels com - in' af - ter me,__

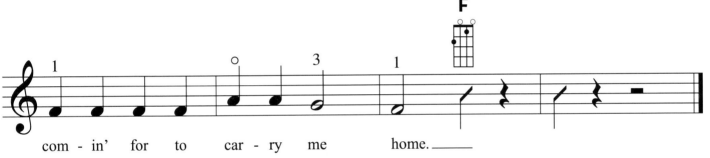

com - in' for to car - ry me home._____

Additional Lyrics

Swing low, sweet chariot,
Comin' for to carry me home;
Swing low, sweet chariot,
Comin' for to carry me home.

If you get there before I do,
Comin' for to carry me home,
Tell all my friends I'm comin' too,
Comin' for to carry me home.

This Little Light of Mine

Book 1, p. 42 (Complete, p. 67)*

Words and music by
Harry Dixon Loes

* This music also correlates to Alfred's Teach Your Child to Play Ukulele, Book 1, p. 83.

I'm gon - na let it shine._____ Let it

shine,_____ let it shine,_____ let it

shine!_____

Additional Lyrics

Won't let Satan blow it out.
I'm gonna let it shine.
Won't let Satan blow it out.
I'm gonna let it shine.
Won't let Satan blow it out.
I'm gonna let it shine.
Let it shine, let it shine, let it shine.

Let it shine 'til Jesus comes.
I'm gonna let it shine.
Let it shine 'til Jesus comes.
I'm gonna let it shine.
Let it shine 'til Jesus comes.
I'm gonna let it shine.
Let it shine, let it shine, let it shine.

Hide it under a bushel - NO!
I'm gonna let it shine.
Hide it under a bushel - NO!
I'm gonna let it shine.
Hide it under a bushel - NO!
I'm gonna let it shine.
Let it shine, let it shine, let it shine.

Let it shine over the whole wide world,
I'm gonna let it shine.
Let it shine over the whole wide world,
I'm gonna let it shine.
Let it shine over the whole wide world,
I'm gonna let it shine.
Let it shine, let it shine, let it shine.

Ukulele Fingerboard Chart
Frets 1–12

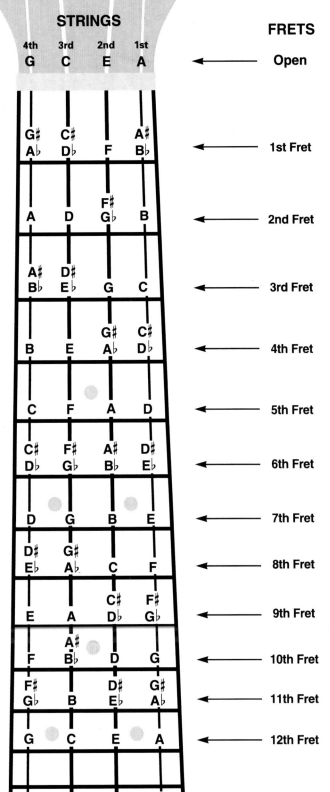

STRINGS				FRETS
4th	3rd	2nd	1st	
G	C	E	A	← Open
G#/Ab	C#/Db	F	A#/Bb	← 1st Fret
A	D	F#/Gb	B	← 2nd Fret
A#/Bb	D#/Eb	G	C	← 3rd Fret
B	E	G#/Ab	C#/Db	← 4th Fret
C	F	A	D	← 5th Fret
C#/Db	F#/Gb	A#/Bb	D#/Eb	← 6th Fret
D	G	B	E	← 7th Fret
D#/Eb	G#/Ab	C	F	← 8th Fret
E	A	C#/Db	F#/Gb	← 9th Fret
F	A#/Bb	D	G	← 10th Fret
F#/Gb	B	D#/Eb	G#/Ab	← 11th Fret
G	C	E	A	← 12th Fret